THE BRILLIANT BOOK OF EXPERIMENTS

ARCTURUS

Picture Credits:

Gianni A. Sarcone and Marie-Jo Waeber: 55. Javier Trueba/MSF/Science Photo Library: 6–7. NASA: 42–43. Ocean/Corbis: 24–25. Photo Researchers/FLPA: 64–65. Pinsharp 3D Graphics: 54. Science Photo Library (Steve Gschmeissner): 82–83. Shutterstock: 22 (Rashevska Natalia), 41, 51, 67 (Thomas M. Perkins), 86, 93, 99, 102–103.

Cover: Shutterstock (center, Morgan Lane Photography; left, Darrin Henry; right Dmitriy Shironosov).

ARCTURUS

This edition published in 2013 by Arcturus Publishing Limited
26/27 Bickels Yard, 151–153 Bermondsey Street,
London SE1 3HA

Editors: Joe Harris and Samantha Noonan
Illustrations: Andrew Painter
Step-by-Step Photography: Sally Henry and Trevor Cook
Science Consultant: Sean Connolly
Layout Design: Orwell Design

ISBN: 978-1-84858-394-8
CH002210US
Supplier 05, Date 0713, Print Run 2741

Printed in Singapore

CONTENTS

CONTINUED ON NEXT PAGE

CONTENTS

MATERIAL WORLD

Everything around you is made of matter. Everything in you is too, imagine that! This chapter is full of facts and experiments exploring the incredible science of materials.

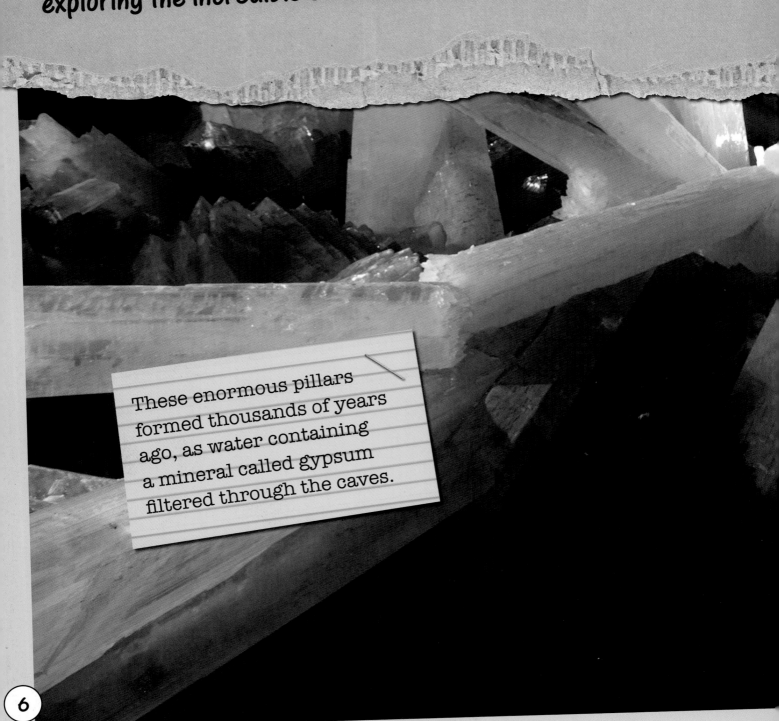

These enormous pillars formed thousands of years ago, as water containing a mineral called gypsum filtered through the caves.

MAKE YOUR OWN LAVA LAMP

Lava lamps are always fascinating to watch. Now you can make your own!

YOU WILL NEED

★ A clean plastic bottle or jar

★ Funnel

★ Vegetable oil

★ Food coloring

★ Effervescent vitamin tablet

★ Flashlight

★ Water

Step 1

Fill a bottle or jar ¼ full with water. Add 10 drops of food coloring.

Step 2

Fill the bottle to the top with vegetable oil.

Step 3

Break the vitamin tablet into four pieces.

Step 4

Drop one piece of the vitamin tablet into the bottle and watch the result.

Step 5

To improve the lava lamp effect, turn off the lights, switch on the flashlight, and shine it through the bottle.

I really "lava" this experiment!

Step 6

Experiment with different jars and bottles and other food colorings. Which work the best?

You can restart your lava lamp by adding another tablet.

HOW DOES IT WORK?

Oil and water do not mix. When you add oil to water it usually just sits on its own in a separate layer on top of the water. However, adding the bit of tablet to the container changes this. The tablet reacts with the water, creating bubbles of carbon dioxide gas which rise to the surface. The oil and water are stirred up by the bubbles.

CANDY VOLCANO

Get ready for an edible eruption! In this experiment, you'll discover that mixing soft-centered mints and diet cola can have explosive results.

YOU WILL NEED

★ Two packets of strawberry flavored gelatin

★ A packet of soft-centered mints

★ Hot water

★ A large mixing bowl

★ A small glass

★ A can of diet cola

★ Plate

★ Tray

Step 1

Take two packets of gelatin. Follow the instructions on the packets to make a gelatin mixture.

Step 2

Take a big bowl. Turn a glass upside down inside it.

Step 3

Pour the gelatin mixture into the bowl. Make sure it covers the glass.

Step 4

Put the gelatin in the fridge to set. When the gelatin has set, turn it out onto a flat plate and remove the glass.

Step 5

Put the plate onto a tray. Take the gelatin outside and pour diet cola into the cavity left by the glass.

Drop six soft-centered mints into the cola. Watch out—it will erupt!

KABOOM!

Add more cola if you want.

This experiment is good enough to eat... if you're brave enough!

HOW DOES IT WORK?

The bubbles in a cola drink are made up of carbon dioxide gas. They have been forced into the drink under pressure. When you drop a soft-centered mint into the soda, the carbon dioxide bubbles collect together and grow in the tiny dents on the surface of the mint. Then the bubbles rush out in an eruption.

MAKE A BALLOON KEBAB

You can't stick a sharp object through a balloon without popping it. Right? Wrong! Amaze your family and friends by making a genuine balloon kebab.

Step 1

Blow up a balloon to about half its full size, and tie a knot in the neck.

No one will believe these results—but it really works!

Step 2

Hold the balloon in one hand and the kebab skewer in the other.

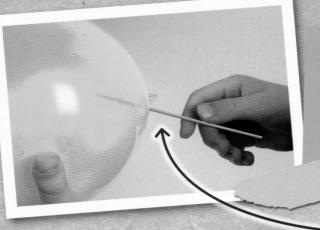

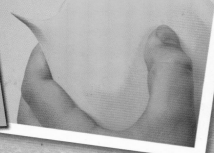

Step 3

Poke the point of the skewer into the the balloon, near the knot.

Wipe a little vegetable oil on the skewer, so that the skewer slides in smoothly.

Step 4

Push the skewer through the balloon very gently, twisting as you push. Aim to make it come out on the opposite side, at the middle of the top of the balloon.

Step 5

If you have a long skewer, or small balloons, try to add more balloons—like a kebab!

Step 6

If you poke the balloon in the middle with the skewer, it will pop.

HOW DOES IT WORK?

Normally, when a balloon is stabbed with a kebab skewer, the rubber skin will tear and it will pop. That is because the pressurized air inside the balloon is stretching the skin very tight, so that the slightest hole blows open in an instant. However, the skin is not as tight at the "ends" of a balloon. So stabbing it there won't pop it—as long as you're careful.

MAGNETIC CEREAL

Is the iron contained in food the same thing as the metal iron? Try this experiment to find out.

Step 1

Crush some cereal into a fine powder in a small bag.

The bag keeps the cereal together.

Oh no! Keep that magnet away from me!

Step 2

Put the magnet in the powder and roll it around.

Step 3

Take the magnet out of the bag. It should have crumbs of cereal sticking to it.

Try shaking the powder off—the magnetic attraction won't let you!

Step 4

Take a clean cereal bowl and fill it almost to the top with water.

Step 5

When the water has stopped any movement, drop a large flake of cereal on the surface, in the middle of the bowl.

Step 6

By holding your magnet just above the cereal flake, you should be able to draw it across the surface of the water without touching it!

HOW DOES IT WORK?

This experiment shows that fortified cereals, like many other foods, contain iron in small amounts. It is very important that you get enough iron in your diet. Iron helps your blood to carry oxygen around the body. If you don't have enough of it, you may feel tired and unwell.

BUBBLE BOMB!

YOU WILL NEED:

★ Water

★ A measuring cup

★ A sealable plastic bag

★ Paper towel

★ 2 tablespoons of sodium bicarbonate

★ Vinegar

This fun and safe "bomb" will explode with a loud pop!

Step 1

Find a place where making a mess won't be a disaster—outside, or perhaps the bathroom if the weather's bad.

Step 2

Test your bag for leaks. Put some water in it, close the seal and turn it over. If no water leaks out, it's okay to use.

Get ready for a bubble BOOM!

Step 3

Tear a small piece of paper towel, about 5 inches (13 cm) square. Put 2 tablespoons of sodium bicarbonate in the center of the square and fold the paper towel around it.

18

Step 4

Mix 10 fl oz (300 ml) of vinegar and 5 fl oz (150 ml) of warm water and pour them into the plastic bag.

Step 5

Put the paper towel packet into the bag and hold it in the corner away from the vinegar while you seal the bag.

Step 6

Place the bag on the floor and stand well back!

Step 7

The bag will swell up...

Step 8

...and then pop!

HOW DOES IT WORK?

Vinegar is an acid and sodium bicarbonate is a base. When you mix acids and bases together, they react and turn into different chemicals. They usually turn into water and a salt, and in some cases, they also form a gas. When carbon dioxide gas forms in our experiment, there is not enough room for it in the plastic bag. So the pressure builds up and the bag swells until it pops and releases the gas.

GLOOPY GOOP

This strange slime is not really a liquid, but not really a solid either! Make some for yourself to find out what sort of material it is.

Step 1

Pour a cup of cornstarch into a mixing bowl. How does the cornstarch feel?

Step 2

Add two drops of food coloring to the water. You really don't need very much!

Step 3

Mix the water into the flour, using your fingers. How does the mixture feel?

Step 4

Try squeezing a handful of the liquid you've made into a ball. It will become a solid!

Step 5

Let the goop settle into the bottom of the bowl. Touch the surface gently, then tap it hard.

My goop has come to life! I think I'll call him "Bob."

How do you do?

Step 6

If you hold your hand still, it will become liquid and run through your fingers.

HOW DOES IT WORK?

When this mixture is put under pressure, the cornstarch molecules are forced together, and it behaves like a solid. When it is handled gently, the cornstarch molecules can move around freely, and it flows like a liquid.

COIN CLEANER

YOU WILL NEED

★ Dirty coins
★ Cola
★ A plastic cup
★ A paper towel
★ Old toothbrush

Many people like to collect coins from different countries. However, coins tarnish easily, and can soon start to look dirty. Here is how you can give them back their shine.

Step 1

Take some dirty coins. Why not take a photograph to compare results later on?

Step 2

Rinse a coin in water to remove loose dirt.

Step 3

Put the coin in a plastic cup and pour in some cola.

Step 4

After 20 minutes, take the coin out and dry it.

Step 5

Repeat the process until the coin is clean. With a really dirty coin, it may help to agitate the cola on the coin with an old toothbrush.

Step 6

Take pictures of your coin at intervals to see the rate of change. Here's a very dirty old coin, showing results after 30 mins, 2 hours, 6 hours, 12 hours, and a day.

These clean, shiny coins really look like a million dollars!

HOW DOES IT WORK?

Cola drinks are more acidic than you might think! The cola is corroding away the top layer of the coins. That makes them look clean.

PUSH AND PULL

In this chapter, we explore the science of forces. Forces are all around us and are acting on us all the time!

This man is skysurfing high above the earth! This is made possible by the forces of gravity (pulling him down) and air resistance (slowing his fall).

BOOK BATTLE

YOU WILL NEED
- ★ Two phone books or large catalogs with pages made of thin paper
- ★ Two volunteers

This fantastic trick might seem like fiction, but actually it's all about friction!

Tell your friends, "I bet you can't pull these apart!"

Step 1

Take two big, thick books, with plenty of pages.

Step 2

Turn a page from each book alternately so that they overlap by a few inches.

Step 3

Continue until the books are completely combined.

Step 4

Find two volunteers, and ask them whether they think they can pull the books apart. It looks easy, but in fact it is impossible!

HOW DOES IT WORK?

When you slide two pages across each other, a force called friction resists the movement. When all the pages of a book are overlapped as in our experiment, that friction is multiplied by the number of pages. That's a lot of friction—so it's impossible for anyone to pull the books apart!

WEIRD WATER

This fiendishly clever bit of science can be used as a perfect practical joke to play on your friends and family!

YOU WILL NEED:

★ A plastic water bottle

★ Water

★ A thumbtack

★ An outdoor space—this could get messy!

Step 1

Fill a plastic water bottle right to the very top.

Step 2

Screw the cap on firmly.

"Water" great experiment!

Step 3

Make holes around the sides of the bottle with a thumbtack. The water won't come out—yet! Now take your bottle somewhere that you don't mind getting wet.

Step 4

Ask a friend if they would like a drink, and give them the bottle.

Step 5

When they open the lid… the water will pour out of the holes. They're in for a soaking!

Now try this:

Try doing the same experiment with a soft-sided container, like a large plastic bag. Fill the bag with water, hold it up with one hand, and make holes with the thumbtack.

HOW DOES IT WORK?

Water cannot escape through the holes while the lid is on, because the air pressure pushing on the side of the bottle is stronger than the downward pull of gravity on the water. But when the lid is removed, air rushes in and adds its force to gravity's pull…and SPLASH!

MARBLE MADNESS

This is another experiment that can be performed as a magic trick. Tell your family and friends that you are going to pick up a marble in a glass without touching the marble.

Step 1

You will need a wine glass shaped like this.

This part is the bowl. It needs to be wider in the middle than at the rim.

Step 2

Ask a volunteer if they can pick up a marble without touching it or using the glass to scoop it up. They won't be able to!

Step 3

Now show them how it's done. Place the glass over the marble. Hold the glass by the base and start gently moving it in a circular motion.

Step 4

The marble should start rolling around inside the glass.

Step 5

Rolling the marble at the right speed should keep it rotating in the widest part of the bowl. Lift the glass up as you rotate it. Your audience will impressed!

HOW DOES IT WORK?

This experiment is a contest between two forces: gravity and centrifugal force. As long as the marble is rolling fast enough, the centrifugal force pushing it outward to the widest part of the glass will be greater than the gravity pulling it downward. So the marble will roll around the glass rather than dropping out.

This really puts a new spin on gravity!

31

BALANCING BUTTERFLY

Is it possible to balance a piece of paper on a single finger? Sure it is! Here's how to make a beautiful, balancing butterfly.

YOU WILL NEED:

★ Thin cardboard
★ Tracing paper
★ Pins
★ Scissors
★ A black marker
★ Colored markers or paints
★ Pencil
★ Small coins
★ Super glue

Step 1

Draw a butterfly shape on a piece of thin cardboard. The tips of the wings must be above the head.

Step 2

Ink over the lines with a black marker. Decorate the body and wings with colored pens or paints.

Step 3

Cut out the shape with scissors.

Step 4

Fix matching coins to the tips of the wings.

Step 5

Bend the wings down a little.

Step 6

The balance point should be near the head, depending on the weight of your coins and the cardboard thickness.

Step 7

You should be able to balance the butterfly on the tip of your finger!

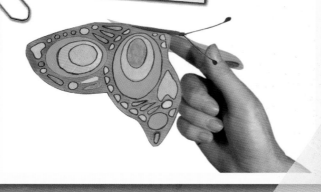

Step 8

You can put butterflies all around the room, on furniture, mirrors, ornaments, flower pots—wherever there's a place for them to balance!

These butterflies make great decorations!

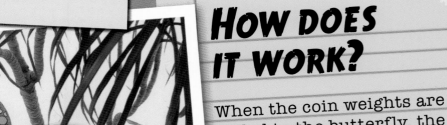

HOW DOES IT WORK?

When the coin weights are added to the butterfly, the center of gravity falls almost directly between them, which is where your finger is, so it makes it easy to balance.

HOMEMADE COMPASS

You will never be lost again once you know how to make your own compass!

YOU WILL NEED:

★ A glass
★ Water
★ A sewing needle (be careful of the point!)
★ Thin cardboard
★ Scissors
★ A pencil
★ Colored markers
★ A bar magnet

Step 1

Hold a needle in one hand and stroke the north end of a magnet along its length 50 times, from point to eye.

Make strokes like this.

Step 2

Using scissors, cut a piece of thin cardboard in an arrow shape, just a little longer than your needle.

Step 3

Thread the needle through the thin cardboard, making sure the point is at the same end as the arrow.

Step 4

Fill a glass with water.

Step 5

Gently lower the arrow onto the water.

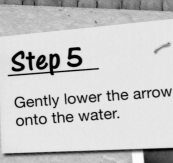

Step 6

The arrow should point north!

If the arrow is pointing south, you may have used the wrong end of the magnet in step 1!

Step 7

Now that you know which direction is north, write all the compass points on a piece of cardboard, just a little larger than your glass.

Now that we have a compass, we just need a treasure map!

Place your glass on top of this card.

HOW DOES IT WORK?

When you rub the needle with the magnet, it becomes a weak magnet itself and will automatically point to the magnetic north pole. Floating it on the water reduces the friction, allowing the needle to easily turn around to point in the direction it is attracted to.

35

WOBBLER TOY

This wobbler toy makes a great gift! No matter how much it wobbles, it will never fall down.

Step 1

Get an adult to help you cut a table tennis ball in half, using scissors.

Step 2

Cut out a rectangle of paper measuring 5 x 2 inches (125 x 50 mm). Draw a line half an inch (12 mm) from one narrow end.

If you push them over, they bounce right back!

Step 3

Draw a face and body on the paper, like this. We're going to decorate this one as a fairy, but there are other ideas on page 38.

Step 4

Roll the paper into a tube, overlapping as far as the pencil line. Fix it in place with the gluestick.

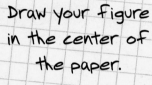

Draw your figure in the center of the paper.

Step 5

Tape one half of the ball to each end. Finish drawing the top of the head.

Step 6

She won't stand up yet!

Step 7

Take the foot end off. Put a lump of modeling clay in the middle of the half ball and and stick it back on the body.

Step 8

Now stand your character up, and try pushing it over.

Step 9

You could make more wobblers and decorate them as aliens or circus performers, or use your own ideas!

Gravity pulls DOWN, but it makes wobblers stand UP!

HOW DOES IT WORK?

The wobbler has a very low center of gravity, because its top half is light but its base is heavy. When another force acts on it (for example, when you give it a push), gravity will pull it back to a point directly above the point where its mass is concentrated. This is called its state of equilibrium.

PARACHUTE JUMP

It's time to parachute some cork commandos behind enemy lines. Which parachute works best?

YOU WILL NEED:

★ String
★ Materials for making the parachutes, such as plastic shopping bags, paper, foil, and tissue paper
★ A pencil and ruler
★ Scissors
★ Tape
★ A cork
★ A small eyehook
★ A kitchen scale
★ A sturdy chair
★ A stopwatch (on a cell phone or wristwatch)

Step 1

Using scissors, cut a 12 inch (30 cm) square from a plastic shopping bag.

Step 2

Cut four pieces of string 12 inches (30 cm) long. Tie one end of each piece of string to a corner of the square of plastic.

Step 3

Twist an eyehook into one end of a cork.

Step 4

Hold the strings from the parachute together, and tie them to the screw.

Step 5

Stand on a chair, reach as high as you can, and drop the parachute.

Ask a friend to time how long the cork takes to fall!

Step 6

Try making parachutes of different sizes and materials. You can also try using other objects as weights, such as plastic toys. Drop them from the same height.

Step 7

Make a chart to see which features make the best parachutes. Time your test drops. Measure the size and weight of the parachute.

Size	Weight	Material	Time

HOW DOES IT WORK?

Parachutes work by creating air resistance. This is a kind of friction which works against the pull of gravity. The best way to increase air resistance is by making as large a surface area as possible. So the size of your parachute will probably make more of a difference than anything else.

BRIGHT IDEAS

In this chapter we will explore the science surrounding the fastest thing in the universe—light! It travels at 186,200 miles per second (300,000 km per second) if you were wondering...

This picture shows a "stellar nursery" far across our galaxy. This is where stars are born and the light takes thousands of years to reach earth. So when you are looking at the stars, you are actually looking at the past!

KALEIDOSCOPE

YOU WILL NEED:

★ A paper towel tube

★ Compass

★ Paper and thin black cardboard

★ A pen or pencil

★ Mirrored cardboard

★ A ruler

★ Scissors

★ Tape

★ Colored tape

★ A thumbtack

★ Plastic wrap

★ Tracing paper

★ Small pieces of colored cellophane

★ Colored wrapping paper

Step 1

Draw around the bottom of a paper towel tube onto a piece of paper. Open your compass so the point is on the circle and the pencil is exactly in the middle. Draw the shape shown with dotted lines. Mark in the base of the triangle, then measure this line. The other two lines of your triangle should be this exact length.

Step 2

Using a ruler, draw a rectangle the same length as the cardboard tube onto the back of the mirrored cardboard. Mark off three parts with the same width as the sides of the triangle you drew.

Step 3

Fold the mirrored cardboard along the lines, to form a triangular shape. The mirrored side should be on the inside. Slide it into the paper towel tube.

Step 4

Draw around the end of the tube onto a piece of black cardboard. Cut out the circle, using scissors.

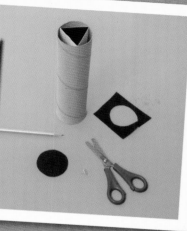

Step 5

Stick the circle on the end of the tube with tape. Make a hole in the center.

Make the hole with a thumbtack.

Step 6

Turn over the tube. Stretch plastic wrap over this end, and fix it in place with tape.

Step 7

Cut a 1 inch- (25 mm-) wide strip of thin cardboard and tape it around the end of the tube. Make sure it stands out a little from the end of the tube.

We finished it off with red tape.

Step 8

Place some small pieces of colored cellophane on top of the plastic wrap.

Soon you'll be watching crazy patterns!

Step 9

Draw around the bottom of the tube onto tracing paper. Cut out the circle, leaving a gap of about half an inch (12 mm). Cut small flaps around the edge. Place this shape over the top of the tube and stick down the flaps with tape.

Step 10

Decorate the tube with colored paper.

Step 11

Hold your kaleidoscope up to the light. Look through the hole and turn the tube. What do you see?

HOW DOES IT WORK?

Light normally travels in a straight line. When it hits a mirror, it bounces off it in a different direction—this is called reflection. In a kaleidoscope, the light bounces around back and forth off the walls, creating many, many reflections of the colorful objects inside.

HALL OF MIRRORS

Have you ever been to the carnival and looked in the crazy mirrors? They can make you look tall, short, wide, slim, or just plain weird! Now you can make your own crazy mirrors at home.

YOU WILL NEED:

★ A big, shiny spoon
★ 2 shallow cardboard boxes (e.g. shoe box lids)
★ Four sheets of thin, mirrored cardboard
★ Tape
★ Scissors
★ A craft knife
★ Mounting putty
★ Thin, black cardboard

Step 1

Look at your reflection in a shiny spoon. What differences can you see between the reflections on each side?

This kind of curved surface is called CONCAVE.

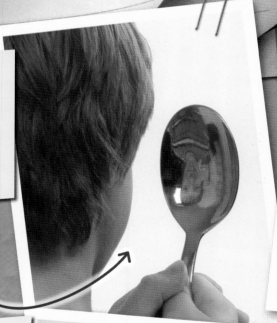

This kind of curved surface is called CONVEX.

Step 2

Let's make some mirrors to see those effects more clearly! Line the sides of a shallow cardboard box with black paper. Strengthen the corners with tape.

47

Step 3

Measure the inside of your box. Then cut a piece of thin, mirrored cardboard or plastic to the same width as the box, but about 2 inches (50 mm) longer.

Step 4

Bend the mirror and place it in the box. The sides should hold it securely.

Step 5

Cut a hole in the bottom of another box with scissors, leaving half an inch (12 mm) around the edge.

Step 6

Prepare the mirrored cardboard as before, but this time turn it the other way up.

Step 7

Ask an adult to help you score some mirrored cardboard in different ways, using a craft knife.

Step 8

Stick the pieces of mirrored cardboard onto a black or colored piece of cardboard, using mounting putty. Decorate the frames with colored paper. Now you have four mirrors ready for your hall of mirrors!

HOW DOES IT WORK?

When light hits the surface of a mirror, the direction of the reflected light depends on the shape of the mirror. If a mirror bulges outward, it is called convex. Convex mirrors make objects look stretched. If a mirror bends inward, it is called concave. Concave mirrors make objects look smaller, or even flip them upside down! It depends on how far away you stand.

Does this reflect well on me?

A BOX FULL OF SKY

Have you ever wondered why the sky is blue when it is lit by the sun, which looks orange? Here is a simple experiment that explains it all.

YOU WILL NEED:

★ A large, clean, glass or plastic container

★ A flashlight

★ A spoon

★ Milk

★ Water

★ Books

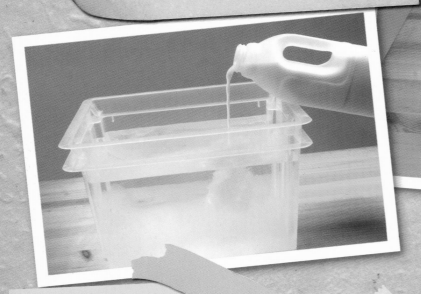

Step 1

Fill the container three quarters full of water. Add a little milk to the water, and stir it with a spoon.

Step 2

Position the flashlight on some books, so that it shines through the the middle part of the water.

Step 3

Shine the flashlight through the water, but stand to the side of the beam. Keep adding milk to the water and stirring. After a while, the light will turn blue.

The milky water in our experiment acts like the sky.

Step 4

Now stand in front of the flashlight. The beam will look orange!

HOW DOES IT WORK?

When the sun shines through the atmosphere, light of different colors is bounced around by air particles. Blue-colored light gets bounced around more than light of any other color, so whichever direction you are looking from, the sky appears blue. The same thing happens in our experiment, when light is bounced around by the milk.

Red and yellow light is bounced around much less than blue, so when you look at the beam of the flashlight, it looks orange. The sun looks orange for the same reason.

3-D GLASSES

View amazing 3-D pictures through your own handmade glasses!

Step 1

Copy the template opposite, and cut out the three parts of the glasses. Score along the dotted lines.

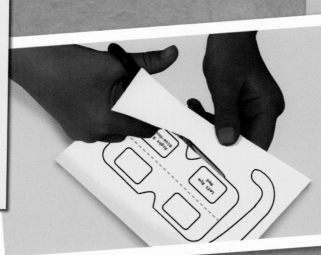

Step 3

Fold the earpiece flaps along the dotted lines and fix to the frame with a glue stick or tape.

Step 2

Cut out two rectangles of colored plastic—one should be blue-green and the other red. Tape them to the glasses.

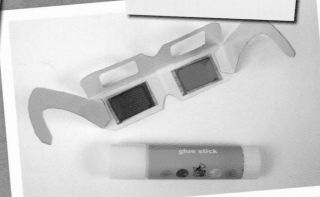

Step 4

Fold the frame down to seal in the lenses and the earpiece flaps. Secure them with tape.

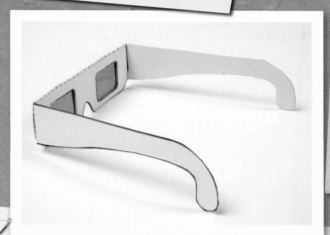

HOW DOES IT WORK?

The blue-green lens makes it hard to see blue and green, but you can still see red. The red lens does the opposite. Your brain tries to make sense of the different images each eye is seeing by turning them into a 3-D picture!

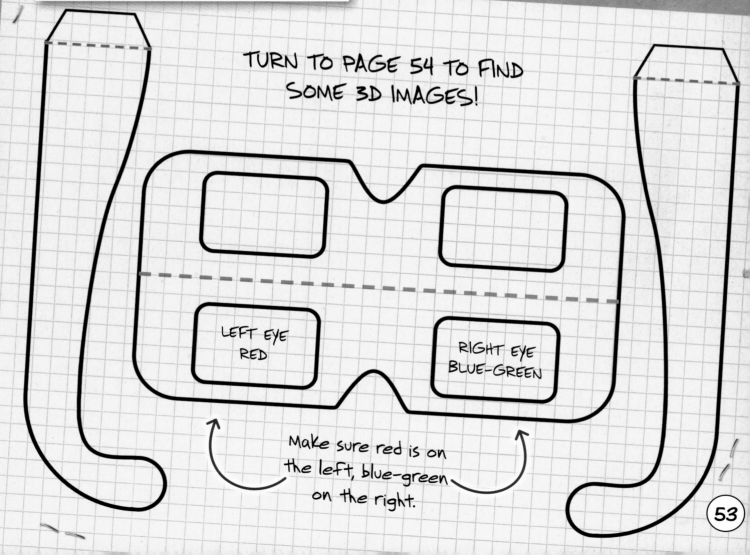

TURN TO PAGE 54 TO FIND SOME 3D IMAGES!

LEFT EYE
RED

RIGHT EYE
BLUE-GREEN

Make sure red is on the left, blue-green on the right.

Wow! It feels like I am really there!

54

TRICK YOUR EYES!

Sometimes what you see is not all it seems. You can play tricks on your brain and eyes with these fun optical illusions!

Step 1

Look at the rabbit in the middle of this picture. Does it look as if the spots are rippling and moving?

HOW DOES IT WORK?

A phenomenon such as an optical illusion tricks us because the different cells and receptors in the eyes receive and process information at different rates. As a result, the brain can sometimes receive a false image based on the information arriving at varying speeds.

Malfunction! My visual systems are not working properly.

LIGHT TOP

Make a terrific top that changes color before your eyes as it spins around!

YOU WILL NEED:
- ★ Old CDs or DVDs
- ★ Marbles
- ★ Tape
- ★ A hard surface
- ★ A pencil
- ★ Scissors
- ★ Pens or paints
- ★ Colored paper

Step 1

Draw round a CD or DVD on colored paper. Cut out several circles. Also cut out the holes in the middle.

Did someone say "marbles?" I lost mine years ago!

Step 2

Stick a paper disk to the CD or DVD with a gluestick.

Step 3

Fix a marble in the central hole of the disk with small strips of tape. Test spinning it on a hard surface, such as a kitchen worktop.

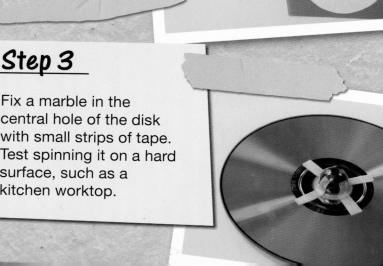

Step 4

Use more paper or colored pens or paints to make bold patterns on the disk.

Can you see new colors when the disk spins?

Step 5

Now try spinning your first disk.

Step 6

Here are some patterns to copy. Or you could make up some of your own!

Step 7

Here's a way to make neat segments.

Fold a circle three times. Then cut along the last fold with scissors.

HOW DOES IT WORK?

When the top whirls around really fast, you can see all the colors, but your brain can't separate them. So what you see is a blend of all the colors mixed together.

What happens if you make a spiral pattern?

MAKE YOUR OWN ZOETROPE

Have you ever dreamed of being an animator? You can make a start here by creating your first ever moving picture!

YOU WILL NEED:

★ A circular box (such as a cheese box) with a lid
★ Modeling clay
★ A push pin
★ A small button
★ A piece of cork
★ Tape
★ A ruler
★ A pencil and pen
★ Black paper and white paper
★ Colored paper or tape

Step 1

Poke a hole in the center of a circular box and its lid with a push pin.

Use a ruler to find the exact center.

Step 2

Put some modeling clay around the edge of the inside of the box, to add weight.

Zoe Trope? I think I went to school with her.

59

Step 3

Push the map pin through the lid, through the hole in a button, through the bottom of the base, and into a cork beneath. The box should now spin freely on the lid.

Step 4

Cut a piece of black paper about 2.5 inches (65 mm) high which will fit around the inside edge of the lid.

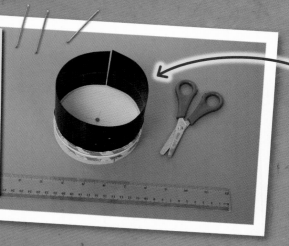

Trim the paper to exactly fit the lid.

Step 5

Draw lines along the black paper about 1 inch (30 mm) apart. Following those guidelines, cut slots about 1.5 inches (40 mm) deep.

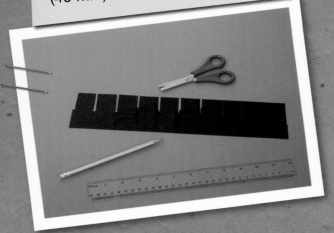

Step 6

Stick the black paper in place with tape. Then cut a piece of white paper, about 1 inch (25 mm) wide, to fit inside it. Don't stick it down yet!

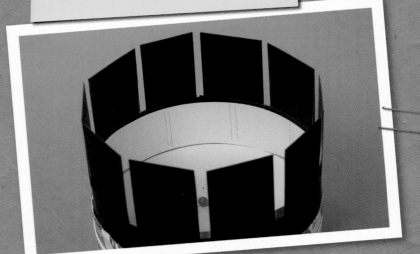

Step 7

Draw guidelines along the white paper about 1 inch (25 mm) apart. Draw a series of pictures in the "frames" you have marked out. Put the paper inside the box.

A repeated action that joins up at the beginning and end will work well.

Step 8

Spin the zoetrope and watch your animation through the slits.

You could decorate the outside of the box with colored paper or tape.

HOW DOES IT WORK?

When you spin the zoetrope, you can see each of the pictures one at a time in very quick succession. Your brain tries to make sense of what your eyes take in. It interprets these rapidly changing pictures as movement, so you see a continuous moving picture.

RAINBOW MAKER

You don't need to wait for rain to see a rainbow anymore. Here is how to make a nice, dry one indoors. You may not find a pot of gold at the end, though!

YOU WILL NEED:

★ Some old CDs

★ A sunny day, or if this is not possible, a flashlight

★ A window with curtains or blinds

★ White paper

Step 1

Find a sunny window. Close the blind or curtain, but leave a little gap to let a direct sunlight in.

Step 2

Hold a CD, shiny side up, in the beam of sunlight.

My pet chameleon just loves rainbows.

Step 3

Reflect the light onto a piece of white paper.

Step 4

Change the angle of the CD. You will see a variety of different rainbow patterns.

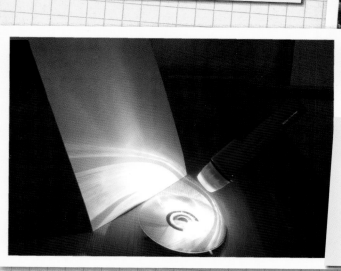

Step 5

You can use a flashlight if it's not a sunny day, but the rainbows might not be as bright.

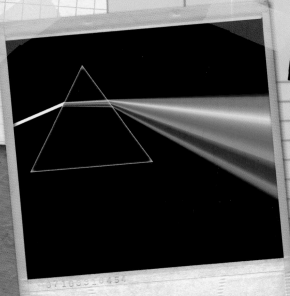

HOW DOES IT WORK?

When white light passes through a triangular prism, it splits into all the different colors of the rainbow. The surface of a CD is made of plastic with lots of tiny ridges above a mirrored surface. These act like lots of tiny prisms arranged in a circle, so when light hits the surface of the CD, it makes a rainbow.

IT'S ALIVE

The world is full of fascinating and amazing living things. From bugs to birds to your own body, get ready to dive in and explore!

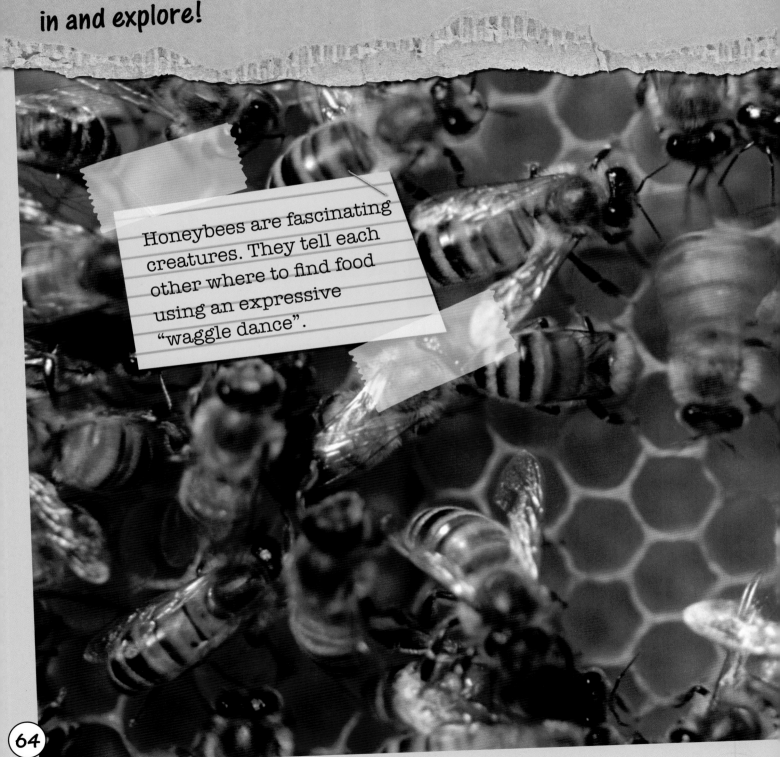

Honeybees are fascinating creatures. They tell each other where to find food using an expressive "waggle dance".

YEAST BALLOON

Yeast is a tiny microorganism that has a massive impact on your life. See the amazing power of yeast by using it to blow up a balloon.

Step 1

Pour 10 fl oz (300 ml) of water into a bowl. Add a packet of dry yeast and 2 tablespoons of sugar and stir the mixture until the yeast and sugar have dissolved.

Step 2

Pour the mixture into the bottle.

Step 3

Warm up the balloon in your hands. To soften the rubber more, grip the ends of the balloon and stretch it.

Will your yeast "rise" to the challenge?

Step 4

Stretch the open end of the balloon over the neck of the bottle. Make sure it is pulled down over the screw threads on the top of the bottle to prevent air from leaking.

Step 5

Leave the bottle upright with the balloon fitted for one hour, then check the result!

Step 6

Leave the bottle undisturbed overnight. In the morning the balloon will be even bigger!

HOW DOES IT WORK?

The yeast needs sugar and water to activate it and it begins to respire (breathe). As it does this, it creates the gas carbon dioxide, which is what blows up the balloon. Yeast is what we use to make bread rise, so it is a very important little creature!

SILLY CELERY

Have you ever seen a plant with blue leaves? Here's how you can dye plants different colors.

YOU WILL NEED:

★ Sticks of celery with leaves still on
★ 2 small glasses
★ 2 bottles of food coloring
★ Water
★ A work top or table
★ Kitchen scissors

Does a celery seller earn a good salary?

Step 1

Pour water into a glass so it is a third full. Add a small amount of food coloring.

Step 2

Trim the bottom of a stick of celery so that it is about 6 inches (15 cm) long. Leave the leaves on.

Step 3

Put the end of the celery into the liquid in the glass. Leave the glass in a safe place, where it won't be moved.

Step 4

Ater one day, cut across the base of the celery with scissors. You will see lines of color rising up the stalk.

Step 5

Split another stick of celery. Put colored water in two glasses. Allow each part of the split stalk to stand in a glass.

Step 6

The following day you will have multicolored celery! Cut back the stalks to check.

HOW DOES IT WORK?

Plants take up water from the soil through their roots. The water travels all the way up the stems to the leaves, through tubes called the xylem. If you put dye in the water, then that will be taken up too. Try the experiment with a white flower to see the petals change color!

HOW BIG ARE YOUR LUNGS?

I'll huff and I'll puff and I'll...test my lung capacity! Try out this simple experiment to see exactly how much air your lungs can hold.

YOU WILL NEED:

★ An empty 2-liter plastic bottle
★ A medium-sized bowl
★ A big bowl
★ A bendy straw
★ Water
★ Lots of puff!

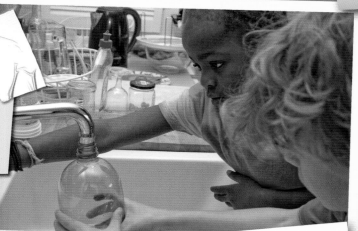

Step 1

Fill a bottle with water right to the top.

Step 2

Screw the cap on.

It is possible to increase your lung capacity with practice.

Step 3

Put the smaller bowl in the bigger bowl. Add water to the smaller bowl until it is ¾ full.

Step 4

Hold the bottle in the bowl with the neck in the water and take off the cap.

Step 5

Take a deep breath!

Step 6

Put the end of the straw in the bottle and blow out one big breath!

Keep the neck of the bottle under the water!

Step 7

You will be able to see how much air you can store in your lungs! Ask a friend or family member to try the experiment. Who has the biggest lung capacity?

HOW DOES IT WORK?

When you blow down, the air you breath out forces out the water that was in the bottle. The empty space is exactly equal to how much air your lungs can hold.

BENDING A CHICKEN BONE

Everybody knows that bones are hard. Or are they? Freak out your family and friends by turning a chicken bone soft and rubbery.

Step 1

Save the bone from a drumstick after a chicken meal.

Step 2

Remove any meat from the bone and rinse it under running water.

What a great excuse for a barbecue!

Step 3

Notice how hard and stiff the bone is. Bones contain a mineral called calcium to make them hard.

Step 4

Put the bone in the jar, then pour vinegar in so it covers the bone completely.

Now you have to wait for the "magic" to happen...

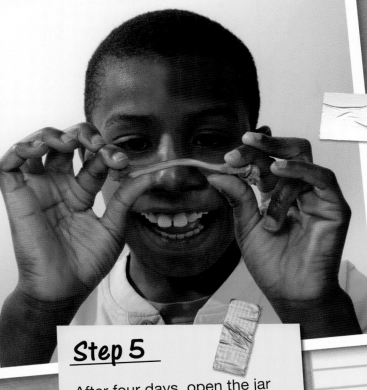

Step 5

After four days, open the jar and take out the bone. Rinse it with water and see how bendy it is! Pour the vinegar away down the sink.

HOW DOES IT WORK?

The vinegar dissolves the calcium in the bone. The calcium is what made the bone strong and hard and without it, the bone becomes soft and bendable. This is why it's important for you to get enough calcium in your diet—trying to walk around with bendy bones wouldn't be much fun!

FOOD ON THE FLY

Attention all animal lovers! These ingenious feeders will attract birds and squirrels to your garden. Then you can observe them and learn all about them!

BOTTLE BIRD FEEDER

YOU WILL NEED:

★ A 2-liter plastic bottle

★ Plastic milk or yogurt containers

★ String

★ Birdseed

★ Scissors

Step 1

Ask an adult to help you cut a circular hole about 2 inches (5 cm) across in the side of a 2-liter bottle, using scissors.

Sometimes squirrels will also eat birdseed.

Step 2

Tie some string around the top of the bottle.

Step 3

Pour some birdseed into your bottle. The seed should nearly reach the hole when the bottle stands upright.

Step 4

Hang up your bird feeder bottle outside where the birds can feed safely. It needs to be high, so they won't feel threatened by cats and other predators.

PEANUT CONES AND POPCORN TREATS

YOU WILL NEED:

- ★ A pinecone
- ★ String
- ★ Peanut butter
- ★ A spoon
- ★ Birdseed
- ★ Popcorn
- ★ Needle and thread

That doesn't look like a tasty treat to me...

Step 1

Tie a piece of string to the top of a pinecone.

Step 2

Smother the pinecone in peanut butter, using a spoon. Then roll it in birdseed and hang it up in the garden.

If your bird feeder starts to look old or get moldy, recycle it and make a nice new one!

Step 3

Get an adult to help you prepare some plain popcorn, then use a needle and thread to join about 50 pieces of popcorn together. Hang it up outside. The birds will love it!

HOW DOES IT WORK?

If you hang your feeders within view of your window, you can observe the birds from indoors so they aren't disturbed. A lot of people put feeders out to help the birds make it through the cold winter, when it can be hard for birds to find food. Watch carefully and see if you can identify different species. See how they interact with each other. Is there a pecking order?

Plain popcorn is very healthy, as well as delicious.

DNA FROM STRAWBERRIES

DNA is the thing that makes you YOU. It is found in every one of your cells, and contains the instructions that your body has followed to make you the way you are. Every living creature has different DNA. Now you can see the DNA of strawberries in your own kitchen!

YOU WILL NEED:

★ A freezer

★ 3 strawberries and salt

★ A measuring cup

★ Scissors

★ A paper kitchen towel

★ A plastic bag

★ 2 plastic cups

★ Laundry detergent (liquid or powdered)

★ A glass

★ Ice cubes

★ 2 big bowls

★ A fork and a teaspoon

★ A toothpick

★ Ice-cold rubbing alcohol (ask an adult for help)

Step 1

Put the rubbing alcohol in the freezer at least an hour before you do this experiment.

Step 2

Remove the stems from the strawberries and break them up using a fork.

Step 3

Put the pieces into a measuring cup. Add one teaspoon of detergent to half a cup of warm water and pour the mixture over the fruit.

Step 4

Stand the cup in a bowl of warm water. The detergent and warm water will start breaking up the strawberry cells. Wait 12 minutes, stirring often.

Step 5

Next, stand the cup in a bowl of ice cubes for 5 minutes.

Want some strawberry DNA with that?

Step 6

Cut the corner off the plastic bag and line it with the paper towel. Then pour the strawberry mush through so the liquid containing the DNA collects in a cup.

Step 7

Add a quarter teaspoon of salt to the collected liquid and mix it well.

Step 8

Now pour some of the mixture into a clear glass, so it is about a third full. Ask an adult to pour in an equal amount of ice-cold rubbing alcohol, and then rock the glass gently.

Step 9

Let the glass stand for a few minutes. A cloudy patch should form at the top of the mixture. It may look bubbly or whiteish. This is strawberry DNA! You can remove it with a toothpick. It will look like clear slime! Isn't it incredible to think that the slime contains all the information for making a strawberry plant?

HOW DOES IT WORK?

To get to a strawberry's DNA, first we mash the fruit to break open its cells. Then we separate the cells into their parts, using the enzymes in washing detergent. The ice stops the detergent from breaking apart the DNA itself. Then we filter the mixture, and the liquid we are left with is called the "supernatent," which contains the DNA. Finally, adding salt and rubbing alcohol makes the DNA break apart from the rest of the solution and rise to the top.

BUG HUNTERS

YOU WILL NEED:
★ A small patch of ground you can dig up
★ Garden trowels
★ A clean jar
★ Grass or leaves
★ A large glass or plastic lid

Time to get up close to some creepy crawlies! They might not be the most pleasant of creatures, but these little guys are a very important part of nature.

There are hundreds of insects under our feet!

Step 1

Find a flat area of ground where you have permission to dig. Make a hole with a trowel, deep enough to hold your glass jar upright.

Step 2

Put some grass and leaves in the hole.

Step 3

Place the jar in the hole without a lid, standing upright to make a trap.

Step 4

Cover the trap with grass and leaves.

Step 5

Protect the trap from the rain by covering the hole with with a glass or plastic lid.

Step 7

Can you identify the bugs and creepy crawlies? Check on the Web or in your library, to find the names and habits of these creatures.

Step 6

Check your trap the following day to see what's in it!

HOW DOES IT WORK?

When bugs fall into your trap, they find it hard to climb back out again because the glass sides are so smooth. See if you can identify the insects that you have caught. Look at them through a magnifying glass to see them in greater detail. Make sure you return the insects to the outdoors when you have had a good look. Leaving insects in the trap for a long time is cruel and could kill them.

SUPER SONIC

Did you know that everything you hear is a vibration? Get ready to learn about the science of sound!

This photo shows the inside of an ear, magnified 21,000 times! Sound vibration makes the liquid in the inner ear move in waves, which makes the hairs sway. They then turn that movement into an electrical signal, which is sent to your brain!

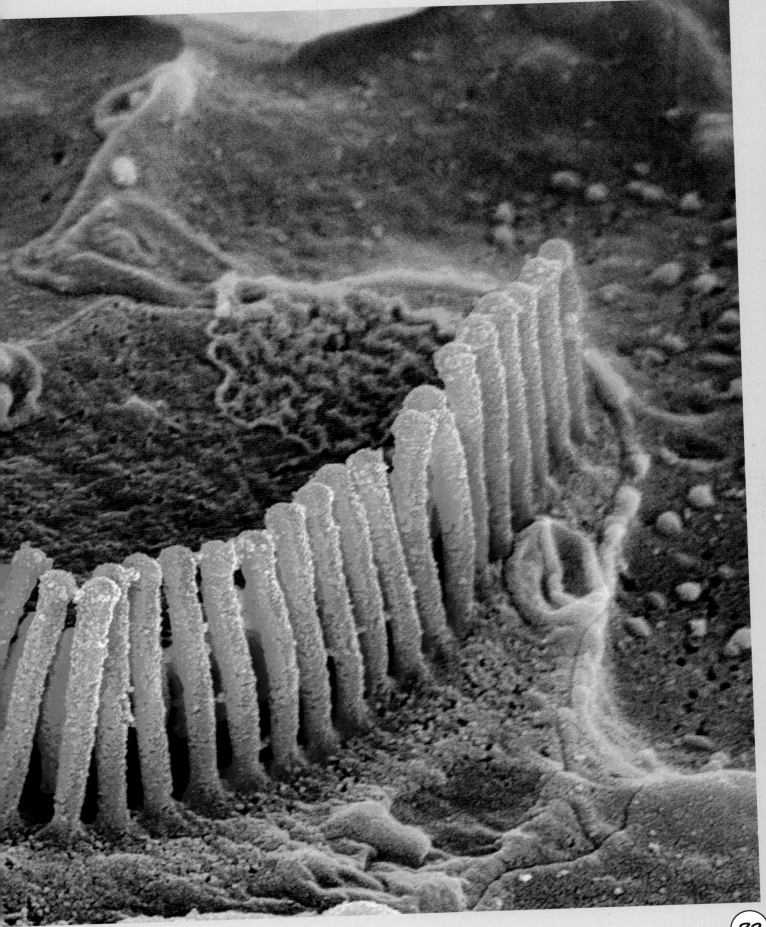

MAKE YOUR OWN DRUM SET

March to the beat of your own drum with this noisy experiment. Using household objects, you can create a drum set that works just like the real thing!

YOU WILL NEED:

★ Containers such as small glass jars, cans, and plastic pails

★ Materials to make the drum skins, such as plastic shopping bags, paper, cloth, aluminum foil, and balloons

★ Materials to make drumsticks, such as chopsticks, cocktail sticks, and wooden spoons

★ A metal saucepan lid

★ Some string

★ Rubber bands

★ Marker pens

★ Scissors

★ Tape and a glue stick

★ Colorful paper

Which containers and drum skins work the best?

We robots love heavy metal!

Step 1

Draw around a can onto a plastic shopping bag. Then cut out the circle with scissors, adding a 0.5 inch (10 mm) margin around the edge.

Step 2

Stick the sheet in place with pieces of tape, pulling the skin tight as you go. Then decorate the can by gluing on colored paper.

You could decorate the drum with the name of your band!

Step 3

Test your first drum with two drumsticks!

Adding tape to the sticks will make a softer sound.

Step 4

Cut down one side of a balloon with a pair of scissors, to make a stretchy skin. Pull it over the top of a small container. Hold it in place with a rubber band.

The rubber band should be tight.

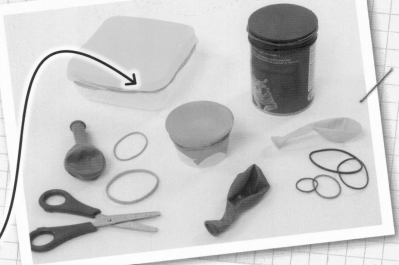

Step 5

Make some more drums from other materials. Each should sound slightly different. Finally, make a cymbal by tying a string around the knob on a saucepan lid. Hang it above the rest of your drum set.

Each drum in a professional drum kit is designed to make a different pattern of vibrations.

HOW DOES IT WORK?

When you hit a drum, it creates a vibration, which is what we hear as a noise. Lots of different things can change the pattern of the vibrations, which changes the noise that you hear: the materials you use, the size of the drum, how tight the skin is stretched, and even where you hit it.

PAPER POPPER

Who knew that a piece of paper could be so LOUD?

YOU WILL NEED:

★ A sheet of paper measuring 16 x 12 inches (400 x 300 mm)

Step 1

Fold the paper in half along the long side, then open it out again.

Step 2

Fold the corners into the crease line in the middle, like this.

Step 3

Fold it again along the original central crease.

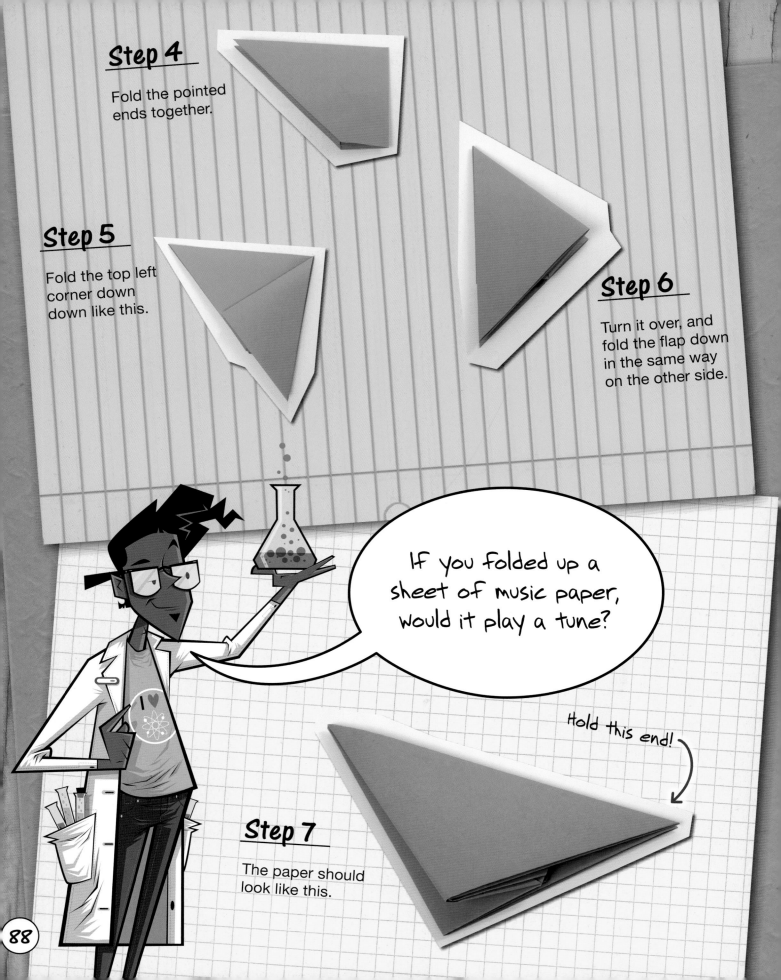

Step 8

Hold the noise maker like this.

Step 9

Swing the noise maker down like this. It should make a sound like cracking a whip!

BANG!

HOW DOES IT WORK?

Swinging the noise maker downward compresses (squashes) the air inside it. The air is suddenly freed when the inner fold opens out. That causes a rapid decompression: a small explosion of air!

DANCING FLAME

We all know you can make a flame flutter by blowing on it, but did you know that you can make a flame dance with the power of sound?

YOU WILL NEED:
* ★ A plastic bottle
* ★ Scissors
* ★ A plastic bag
* ★ A rubber band
* ★ A tea light candle and safety matches

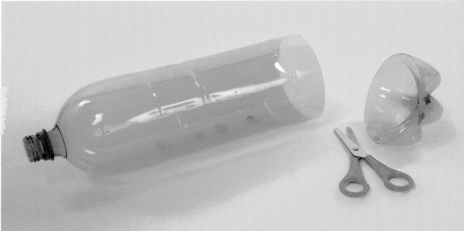

Step 1

Using scissors, cut the bottom off a plastic bottle.

Step 2

Cut a square of plastic from a plastic bag that is at least 0.5 inches (10 mm) bigger than the base of the bottle. Fix it to the base with a rubber band.

WARNING!
Ask an adult to help you with the matches and candle.

Step 3

Light the candle. Position the bottle so the neck points toward the flame.

Step 4

Tap the plastic sheet without moving the bottle. The candle flame will flicker with the sound!

HOW DOES IT WORK?

All sounds are vibrations in the air. We don't normally see what is happening when the air vibrates—we just hear it as the vibrations reach our ears.

However, the small flame in our experiment is so sensitive to air movement that we can clearly see it move in response to vibrations traveling through the air.

Very low-pitched sounds can blow out flames!

FUNKY BONE VIBRATIONS

We already know that vibrations can travel through air. They can also travel through other materials, such as... your head!

Step 1

Bang the fork on a table so that it makes a ringing noise.

Don't risk damaging an expensive table—any hard surface will do.

Step 2

Note how loud the noise is.

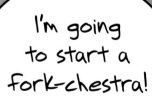

I'm going to start a fork-chestra!

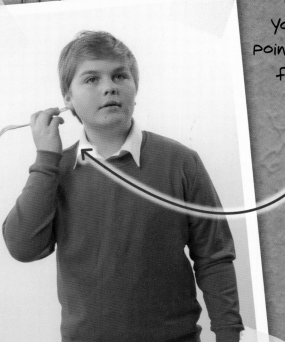

Make sure you hold the pointy end away from you!

Step 3

Now bang the fork again. This time, hold it behind your ear, pressing it against the bone. Is it louder or quieter?

Step 4

Now bang the fork and grip the handle in your teeth. This time it should be really loud!

HOW DOES IT WORK?

This experiment shows you that sound travels better through bone than air. This is important because you have tiny little bones in your ear that vibrate, stimulating nerve signals to the brain to tell you that you are hearing something. If bone didn't conduct sound so well, you wouldn't be able to hear as well as you do.

WHERE'S THAT SOUND?

Why do we need two ears, and not just one? This fun experiment shows you why, by confusing your sense of hearing!

YOU WILL NEED:

★ Two pieces of plastic tubing about 20 inches (50 cm) long, from a hardware store.

★ Two funnels

★ Masking tape and scissors

★ A headband

★ An assistant

Step 1

Attach two funnels to pieces of plastic tubing. You might need to hold them in place with tape.

Step 2

Tape the two pieces of tubing together.

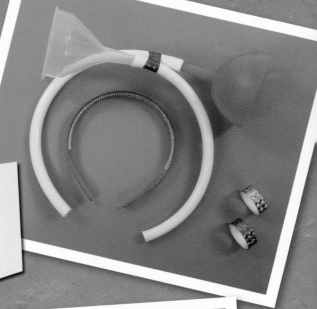

Step 3

Tape the tubes onto a headband.

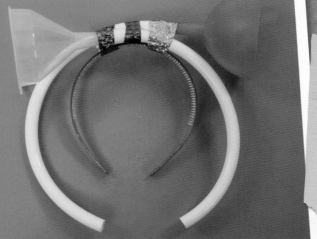

94

Step 4

Put the headset on your head, and hold the ends of the tubes, one in each ear.

Step 5

Close your eyes. Ask your assistant to make a variety of noises in different places.

Step 6

Can you tell where each noise was coming from?

The headset device confuses your brain by making it seem that your ears have swapped sides.

You will almost certainly get it wrong!

HOW DOES IT WORK?

We can normally tell whether a sound is to our left or right based on how loudly we hear it in each ear. The tubes take sounds to the wrong ears!

PAPER KAZOO

Here is how you can make the simplest, silliest instrument in the world. All you need is a simple piece of paper!

Step 1

Rule a line on a piece of paper about 1 inch (2.5 cm) wide and about 4 inches (10 cm) long. Then cut the shape out with scissors.

Step 2

Fold the paper in half lengthwise.

Step 3

Fold the ends back like this.

Step 4

Using scissors, cut a small, V-shaped notch into the middle of the central fold.

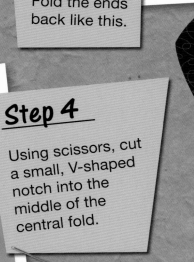

Step 5

Hold it to your mouth like this and squeeze air between your lips.

Step 6

Try making longer and shorter kazoos! Does the sound change?

Step 7

Can you play a tune with your kazoos? Get your friends to join in!

Kazoos are named after the noise they make!

HOW DOES IT WORK?

Blowing between the two sheets of paper makes them vibrate and creates the buzzing sound that you can hear. Reed instruments such as saxophones and clarinets work in exactly the same way.

CUP SCREECH

This experiment might make your friends block their ears! It makes a very loud noise—a noise that drives some people up the wall.

YOU WILL NEED:

★ A piece of string about 15 inches (38 cm) long

★ A plastic cup

★ An old ballpoint pen

★ An eraser

★ Some water

This sound will make your hair stand on end!

Step 1

Make a hole in the bottom of a plastic cup, using an old ballpoint pen.

Place the eraser under the cup to support it as you make the hole.

Step 2

Thread the string through the hole, and tie a knot in the end to stop it coming out.

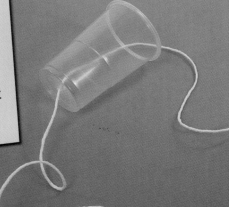

Step 3

Wet the string with water.

Step 4

Hold the cup in one hand like this.

Step 5

With your other hand, slide the wet string between your thumb and forefinger.

With a little practice, you should be able to make a horrible screeching sound!

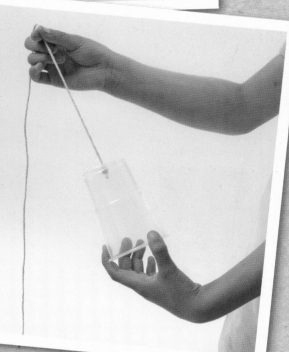

HOW DOES IT WORK?

Your fingers sliding across the wet string make it vibrate and the cup amplifies this, creating a screeching noise. Why do we find this screeching unpleasant? Some scientists think that it is because it is similar to the sound of a scream.

MAGIC RING

YOU WILL NEED:
- ★ Two wine glasses
- ★ A toothpick
- ★ Some water

Gather your friends to watch you perform this awesome magic trick, made possible by the power of sound.

Step 1

Fill both glasses three quarters full of water.

Step 2

Gently rub a wet finger around the rim of each glass. With a little practice, you can make a strange, ringing sound.

Step 3

Adjust the amount of water in each glass until the pitch of the sound made by each glass is the same.

Step 4

When the pitch is the same in both glasses, place them together so they are close, but not touching.

ERROR! ERROR! This magic trick does not compute!

Step 5

Carefully balance a toothpick on the rim of one of the glasses.

Step 6

Wet your finger again and rub it round the rim of the other glass, making the ringing sound. The toothpick will move!

HOW DOES IT WORK?

Because the two glasses contain the same amount of water, they vibrate at the same frequency. Your rubbing creates vibrations, which cause one glass to ring and the other to vibrate and move the toothpick.

HOT STUFF

Temperature can completely change the behavior of the materials around us, and in some cases it can transform them completely. It's time to learn about the science of heat and cold!

Did you know that hot air is lighter than cold air? That is how a hot air balloon flies!

MINI MELT

In this chilly experiment, you can create a miniature iceberg to see how the density of water changes with temperature.

YOU WILL NEED:
* ★ Water
* ★ A small pitcher
* ★ A glass
* ★ Food coloring
* ★ ⅓ cup of vegetable oil
* ★ An ice cube tray
* ★ A freezer

Step 1

Prepare some special ice cubes by adding a few drops of food coloring to some water in a pitcher.

I only seem to have green coloring. Will that do?

Step 2

Fill an ice tray with the colored water, put it in the freezer. It should be frozen in 2 to 3 hours.

Step 3

Fill a glass 1/ full with water.

Step 4

Pour in some vegetable oil until the glass is ²/₃ full.

The water and oil form separate layers.

Step 5

Take an ice cube out of the tray and put it in the glass.

Step 6

Watch as the ice cube melts. What is happening?

Step 7

After about 30 minutes, the ice cube melts completely, the colored cold water stays at the bottom of the glass, and the oil is clear.

HOW DOES IT WORK?

When water is in its liquid form, it is denser than oil, so the oil floats on top of it. However, when the water is frozen and becomes ice, it is less dense than the oil, so the ice floats on top of the oil.

HOMEMADE SHRINK RAY

Put your mad scientist hat on as you use the power of science to shrink everyday objects!

YOU WILL NEED:

- ★ An oven
- ★ An oven mitt
- ★ A timer
- ★ Snack bags (such as potato chip bags) made of plastic—not foil
- ★ Dishwashing liquid
- ★ A paper towel
- ★ Aluminum foil
- ★ Brooch pins
- ★ Super glue

Step 1

We are going to turn a full-size snack bag into a miniature one! Rinse out a snack bag with water and dishwashing liquid. Then ask an adult to preheat the oven to 475°F (245°C).

Step 2

Dry the bag with a paper towel.

Make sure you get rid of all the crumbs and grease.

107

Step 3

Wrap the bag in aluminum foil.

Step 4

Fold over the ends to make an envelope.

Step 5

Ask an adult to help you place the aluminum foil envelope on the top shelf of the oven. Then close the oven door and check the temperature. Set the timer for two minutes. You need to stick to this time exactly.

We're turning trash into cool stuff with the power of heat!

Step 6

After two minutes, ask an adult to help you remove the envelope from the oven using an oven mitt. Place the envelope on a heatproof surface.

Step 7

Pat down the foil envelope with the oven mitt and then let it cool.

Step 8

Once it is cool, remove the shrunken bag from inside.

Step 9

Make gifts for your friends! Attach a brooch pin to the back of the miniature bags to make buttons.

You can try shrinking some other types of snack bags.

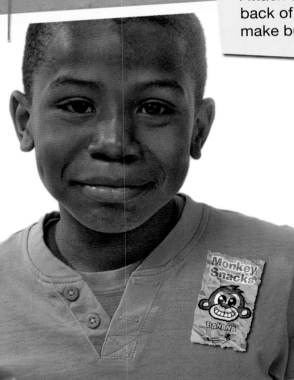

HOW DOES IT WORK?

The molecules making up the bag are in long chains called polymers, which are knotted tightly together. When the bag was made, it was heated and the polymers were stretched out flat. Heating the empty bag up releases the polymers, so they can scrunch up again.

SOLAR STILL

If you were ever stranded in the wilderness, this cool experiment could save your life by creating drinkable water from salt water!

Step 1

Put some salt in a pitcher of water. Add about 4 tablespoons of salt to 1 quart (1 liter) of water. Stir thoroughly.

Step 2

Pour enough salty water into a large bowl so that it is about 2 inches (5 cm) deep.

Step 3

Place the small jar or glass in the center of the bowl of water. Make sure the top of the jar is above the salt water, but well below the top of the large bowl. You'll probably need to put some small, clean stones or marbles in the glass to weigh it down and stop it floating in the water.

Step 4

Stretch some plastic wrap over the top of the large bowl and make an airtight seal.

Step 5

Place a marble in the center of the plastic wrap, directly over the jar to make the plastic slope down into the middle.

Step 6

Put your solar still outside in the sun. Leave it for at least 4 hours. The longer you leave it out, the more water you'll collect.

This experiment is marble-lous!

Step 7

When you are ready to check your solar still, take off the plastic wrap and look at the water that's collected in the jar. Do you think it's salty or fresh? Taste it and see!

HOW DOES IT WORK?

The heat from the sun causes water to evaporate from the bowl, leaving the salt behind. As this happens, the water vapor hits the plastic wrap and condenses back into liquid water again. The marble weighing the plastic down makes the water run down into the jar, thereby allowing you to collect fresh water!

FEELING HOT AND COLD

Why is it that people feel temperature differently? When some people are snuggled in coats, other people are walking around in T-shirts. This experiment tests how this is possible.

Step 1

Pour cold water and ice cubes into a bucket.

Step 2

Pour hot (not boiling) water into another bucket.

Step 3

Fill a large bowl with water at room temperature.

Step 4

Put one hand in the hot water and the other hand in the cold water. Your hands should stay in the water for a few minutes.

Step 5

Take your hands out and plunge them both into the bowl of water at room temperature. The hot hand will feel cold and the cold hand will feel hot!

HOW DOES IT WORK?

This experiment proves that how we feel temperature is relative. If you have just been in a warm place, room temperature might feel quite cool, but if you have been in a cold place, room temperature will feel lovely and warm.

The hot water should be bearable to touch–don't burn yourself!

Step 6

Take your hands out of the water and dry them.

113

ICE CREAM IN A BAG

Here is a simple way to make ice cream in just ten minutes—you'll never chase after the ice cream truck again!

Finally! An experiment that's good to eat!

Step 1

Pour ½ cup whole milk or cream, 1 tablespoon of sugar, and ½ teaspoon of vanilla flavoring into a small sealable freezer bag.

Step 2

Push out as much air as possible as you seal the bag.

Step 3

Place the first bag inside the second small bag, squeezing out the air.

Step 4

Seal the second bag.

Watch your fingers! And be careful with the table too!

Step 5

Make some crushed ice. Fold the ice cubes in a clean towel and beat with a wooden rolling pin on a hard surface.

Step 6

Put the crushed ice in the large freezer bag and add a tablespoon of salt.

Step 7

Put the smaller bags into the middle of the crushed ice and salt mixture in the large freezer bag. Squeeze out as much air as possible and then seal the bag.

Time to get the woolly gloves on!

Step 8

Wearing the gloves, shake and squish the bag so that the ice surrounds the mixture. It should take 5 to 10 minutes for the mixture to become ice cream!

Mmmmm. Yummy!

HOW DOES IT WORK?

The salt lowers the freezing point of the ice. This means it melts faster. When it melts, it takes in energy in the form of heat from the surrounding environment—in this case, the ice cream mixture, which cools it down until it freezes.

SOLAR OVEN

Harness the power of the sun to make tasty treats for you and your friends!

YOU WILL NEED:

* ★ An empty pizza box
* ★ Black water-based paint
* ★ A paint brush
* ★ A black polyethylene bag
* ★ Aluminum foil
* ★ Plastic wrap
* ★ A glue stick, tape, scissors, and a ruler
* ★ A marker pen
* ★ Marshmallows, chocolate, and cookies
* ★ A paper plate
* ★ A wooden stick
* ★ A warm, sunny day!

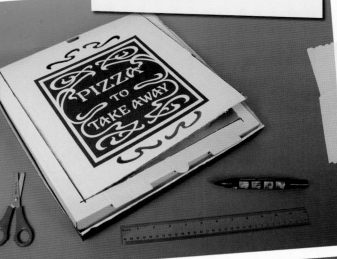

Step 1

Paint the bottom and the sides of the outside of a pizza box black. Allow the paint to dry.

Step 2

Draw a 1 inch (25 mm) border on the front and sides of the top of the pizza box. Cut along the line with scissors.

Step 3

Open the flap in the lid of the box. Stick a square of aluminum foil on the inside of the flap with the glue stick.

Step 4

Seal the opening made by the flap with a piece of plastic wrap.

Step 5

Line the inside of the pizza box with a folded black polyethylene bag. Tape it to the sides to keep it in place.

Step 6

Find a sunny spot in the yard. Close the window in the pizza box and prop open the flap with a stick. Adjust the box so that the foil reflects the maximum sunlight through the window into the oven.

Step 7

Your oven is ready—let's make s'mores! Put a cookie on a paper plate and cover with marshmallows and chocolate.

My taste circuits are tingling!

Step 8

Check on progress in the oven every 10 minutes. Make sure sunlight is still reflected into the oven. On a nice, sunny day, it should take about 30 minutes.

HOW DOES IT WORK?

The idea of a solar oven is to capture as much of the sun's heat as possible. The color black absorbs heat, so this makes sure that the cooking area of the box soaks up as much warmth as possible. Silver reflects heat, so the lid is used to gather more of the sun's heat and direct it to the food. The plastic wrap acts like glass in a greenhouse, allowing the light and heat in, but not letting it out again. All three together make a pretty good oven!

SOAP SCULPTURES

Create your own fun soap sculptures just using the microwave!

YOU WILL NEED:

★ 2 or 3 bars of soap—the whipped sort is best, sometimes sold as "luxury soap"

★ A microwave oven

★ An oven mitt

★ Paper plates

★ Plastic lids from aerosol cans

Step 1

Put a bar of soap on a paper plate. Ask an adult to put it in the microwave on a high setting for 1 minute.

Step 2

Watch through the closed door of the microwave. The soap should expand and grow!

Oooh, microwaves. My favorite kind of radiation!

Step 3

After one minute, the soap should have expanded, but if the original bar shape is still visible, microwave it for another 30 seconds.

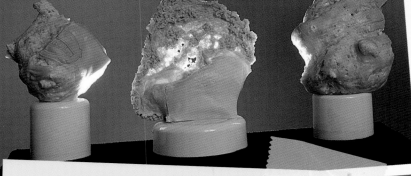

Flatten the bottom of the sculpture so it stands on the plinth.

Step 4

Allow several minutes for the soap to cool before you touch it. Remove it from the microwave with an oven mitt.

Light your finished sculptures in a dramatic way with a desk lamp and take photographs of them!

Step 5

Repeat the process for each sculpture you want to make. Get your friends to make some and see who can get the best results! Make some plinths from aerosol can tops to show off your work.

HOW DOES IT WORK?

When the microwave is turned on, the water molecules in the soap are heated up and turn to vapor. The vapor forms bubbles which expand in the heat, making the soap expand in weird and wonderful ways!

THE JUMPING COIN TRICK

Amaze your family and friends by making a coin jump into the air without touching it!

YOU WILL NEED:

★ A glass bottle with a narrow neck, such as a wine bottle

★ A coin—the right size to fit on the mouth of the bottle

★ Hot water

★ Ice cubes

★ 2 bowls—big enough for the bottle to stand in

Step 1

Put the empty bottle with the lid off in a bowl and pack ice cubes around it. Allow it to cool for a few minutes. While you are waiting, ask an adult to pour some hot water into a bowl.

This is the lazy way to toss a coin.

Step 2

Take the bottle out of the bowl. Put a coin on the mouth of the bottle.

Step 3

Carefully lift the bottle and put it in the bowl of hot water.

Wow! It's like magic!

Step 4

After a little while, the coin jumps off the bottle!

HOW DOES IT WORK?

As the bottle is heated, so is the air inside it. As the air warms up, it starts to expand, pushing on the coin and making it jump.

BALLOON FLAME

YOU WILL NEED:

★ Balloons

★ A candle on a saucer

★ Matches

★ Safety glasses or sunglasses

★ Water

You (and your adult helper) will need nerves of steel to test this fiery experiment!

Get ready to cover your ears!

Step 1

Blow up a balloon and tie a knot in the end.

Step 2

Light a candle and then put on your safety glasses or sunglasses.

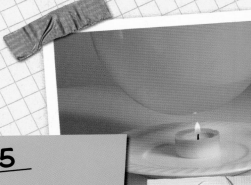

Step 3

Hold the balloon in the flame! What happens?

Step 4

Add some water to another balloon, then blow it up and knot it.

Step 5

Put the part of the balloon holding the water into the flame.

Step 6

After a few seconds, remove the balloon from the flame and examine it!

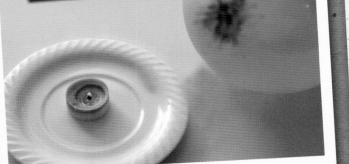

HOW DOES IT WORK?

This is all about the conduction, or transfer, of heat energy. When the balloon is full of air, the candle flame melts the balloon's surface, so it explodes. That's because the heat remains concentrated over the candle. Water conducts heat better than air, so it can absorbe some of the heat—keeping the balloon from melting.

JAR WARS

"Insulators" are materials that stop heat energy spreading. They are used to keep things warm (or cold). This experiment is a hunt for the best insulators.

This certainly is the "coolest" experiment!

Step 1

Check that your jars are clean and that they have lids that fit well.

Step 2

Wrap each jar in a different material, with only one layer of material covering the sides of the jar.

Step 3

Secure the materials with tape but don't cover the tops of the jars. Stand the jars in a row.

Step 4

Fill all the jars with ice-cold water.

Step 5

Record the temperature of the water in each jar. Put all the lids on the water-filled jars. Note the time.

Step 6

Wait five minutes—check the time. Take the temperature again in each jar. Compare the temperatures. Which jar kept the water coldest?

HOW DOES IT WORK?

If you can find a material that is not good at passing heat on, it will be a good insulator. If the heat from the air isn't passed on to the water, the water will remain cold for longer. Which material was the most effective insulator? Can you find another that is better?

GLOSSARY

Air pressure
The force of air as it pushes on things.

Air resistance
A type of friction that slows an object's movement through the air.

Center of gravity
The point that marks the center of an object's mass, so that it acts as a balancing point.

Centrifugal force
The force that draws a rotating object away from the center of rotation.

DNA
A complicated chain of chemicals inside each cell, giving each organism its special qualities.

Enzyme
A chemical that speeds up the way in which substances react with each other.

Equilibrium
Balanced between two or more objects or forces.

Friction
A force that slows moving objects.

Mass
The amount of basic particles that an object has, which on Earth also indicates how heavy that object is.

Microorganism
A living creature that is too small for us to see with the naked eye.

Molecule
A group of atoms bonded together to form what is known a chemical compound. A molecule is the smallest particle that still has all of the chemical properties of a substance.

Polymer
A chemical structure made up of repeating chains of molecules.

Pressurized
Receiving a constant high force.

Xylem
Plant cells that contain tubes to help the plant draw water and other materials upward.

Oh so that's what that word means!